CREATION'S AWESOME CRITTERS

WITH PHIL CALLAWAY

This book is a product of Laugh Again, a ministry of The Good News Broadcasting Association of Canada.
For more products from Laugh Again and Phil Callaway in Canada or worldwide, please visit laughagain.ca, call 1-800-663-2425, or email info@laughagain.ca.
For more products from Laugh Again and Phil Callaway in the United States, please visit laughagain.us, call 1-844-663-2424, or email info@gngm.org.

Content © 2024 Phil Callaway. Publication © 2024 The Good News Broadcasting Association of Canada. Published by The Good News Broadcasting Association of Canada.

ISBN (Paperback) 978-1-998048-13-7   ISBN (Hardcover) 978-1-998048-17-5   ISBN (E-book) 978-1-998048-16-8

CONTENTS

NO BUG IS AN ACCIDENT

Since I was knee-high to our dog Inky, animals have fascinated me. Squirrels. Lizards. Bees. Even cats. I wanted to adopt them all.

Later, when I began to wonder if there really was a God, I looked at my thumb one day, and the thought hit me: *If there is no God, explain this!* I couldn't. Couldn't explain how all these marvels came from nothing. Couldn't explain a sunset or sunrise. Or how the giraffe at the zoo could get a drink without getting his necktie wet. Over time, I began to see that the wonders of heaven and earth could not happen by chance. From the pint-sized to the ginormous, every critter is amazing. Monkeys don't come off an assembly line somewhere. No bug is an accident.

The Lord God made them all.

I almost never use the word "awesome." Why? Because everyone seems to. The word has become ho-hum. **Like tofu! It's bland. Abundant. Always improperly used.** But when I see God at work, there's no better word.

I'm told that if you stack twelve toddlers on an ostrich egg, they won't be heavy enough to break the egg. I have never tried this. But I think that if you pile up these twelve awesome critters, you'll break into a smile. Maybe laugh out loud. And give thanks to their grand and grinning Designer who made you too.

Phil Callaway,
Alberta, Canada

P.S.: A special thanks to my awesome son Steve who helps me write and helps me laugh.

MIRACLE OF MIGRATION

I thought the drone was cool. Then I found out where it came from.

A little girl named Jenny sent me a joke: "Why do birds fly south in winter? Because it's too far to walk."

The sound of music awakes us most summer mornings. It's not the neighbour kids. That would be for the birds, but this is the birds. Robins croon and blue jays shriek their wake up songs at the top of robust lungs.

As we munch our morning toast, we watch them, marveling at what they accomplish waving feathery arms. It doesn't work for humans. I tried it once. From a roof. Don't do this.

From the structure and anatomy of their wings, feathers, and bones, every part of the bird is meticulously designed to take flight. If someone calls you a bird brain, be flattered. Birds' brains are twice the size of human brains in proportion to their bodies. Engineers used birds as a template to design flying machines. But pound for pound, a bird can fly far higher, longer, and further. The amazing bar-tailed godwit can migrate from Alaska to New Zealand without landing for lunch, napping midair. That's 11,700 kilometers in 11 days. Manmade drones of a similar size can fly up to 100 miles.

Then there's the swift. It is designed to fly for nearly ten months without landing. This airborne snacker and sleeper only lands during nesting season to care for its young. In a single year the common swift can cover 200,000 kilometers. In a lifetime, that's enough to fly to the Moon and back five times. Talk about a frequent flyer!

To me, the most impressive bird is also the smallest. When one drops by our house, we stop everything to watch. The average hummingbird weighs about as much as a piece of paper. What they lack in size, they make up for in appetite—eating and drinking multiple times their body weight each day—much like a human teenager.

Resting in a lounge chair, a hummingbird's heart beats 400 times a minute. In the air that jumps to 1,200. Or 20 beats a second. Hatched from a jelly bean-sized egg, they have unique wings that rotate from the shoulder, flapping up to 80 times a second. Hummingbirds can

Four of these facts are true. Can you spot the untruth?

1. Hummingbirds are the only birds that can fly backwards.

2. Blue jays rub ants on their feathers, draining them of acid before gobbling them up. Yum.

3. Swifts eat about 20,000 insects in a day.

4. Dragonflies can see in eight directions at the same time.

5. Some ducks sleep with one eye open.

The fake is #4: They can see in all directions at the same time.

fly upside down, backwards, sideways, and in circles. Where did the template for the humble drone come from? Wonder no longer. Hovering in place, they harvest nectar from flowers by flicking their tongues in and out 13 times a second, remembering yards and blossoms visited the previous year.

This remarkable creature is crafted with love and a twinkle by the Master Designer who invites us to "Look at the birds of the air: they do not sow or reap or store away in barns, and yet your heavenly Father feeds them" (Matthew 6:26, NIV).

So, don't fret or worry, Jenny. That same Creator is with you, loving and watching you. Think of the hummingbird and it might just leave you speechless. Which reminds me of a joke: Why do hummingbirds hum? Because they don't know the words.

"AND GOD SAID... 'LET BIRDS FLY ABOVE THE EARTH ACROSS THE VAULT OF THE SKY.' SO GOD CREATED THE GREAT CREATURES OF THE SEA... AND EVERY WINGED BIRD ACCORDING TO ITS KIND. AND GOD SAW THAT IT WAS GOOD" (GENESIS 1:20-21)

2 GIRAFFIC PARK

The trouble with gravity and how God solved it.

When his Daddy asked our three-year-old grandson Ezra to put the cat outside, he opened the door and said, "Don't worry, Kitty, God will be with you." Children and animals help me laugh. Both provide ample evidence that our Creator God has a sense of humour. Have you seen a naked mole rat? A hairless cat? A proboscis monkey with its wobbly misshapen nose that hangs down past its chin?

The platypus is another amusingly absurd creature. I can just picture God designing the prototype as angels looked on in wonder. "I'll give it a body borrowed from Mr. Beaver, and put flippers on its feet. Then, a duck head. Then have it lay eggs. That will amuse and confuse the humans."

He made the seahorse with the head of a horse and tiny baby fins. The dads give birth! He gave the elephant a seven-foot "nose" with fingers on the end of it so she can grab stuff.

Then there's the implausibly wonderful giraffe. It must be nice being a giraffe. Sure, your jokes go over the other animals' heads, but everyone looks up to you. A giraffe is a great friend. He'll stick his neck out for anyone. With that ginormous neck the terrific giraffe surveys its domain there in Giraffic Park, lunching in the treetops on up to 66 pounds of leaves and twigs a day.

But that neck poses a huge problem when the giraffe has to take a drink. Think about it. In order to sip water, a giraffe's 18-foot high head must descend to the ground. Its 25-pound heart must pump blood *down* the length of its necktie, and when the giraffe stands up that heart must suddenly switch gears and pump *up* against gravity. It's an engineer's worst nightmare. The startling change in pressure would cause humans to pass out and our brains to go "Blam!"

I imagine God smiling and saying, "Well, watch this."

To allow the giraffe to dip up to 20 feet for a satisfying swig and not pass out when it lifts its head back up, a complex system kicks in. Its blood vessels are uniquely designed with reinforced walls and a cushioning web. Sensor signals moderate the pressure. Bypass valves stop the blood from flowing backward and pooling. Did countless giraffes blow their minds before this incredible system evolved? Or was the giraffe miraculously designed with a playful smile and divine blueprints by a loving God?

Water never goes uphill. Ask a plumber. So it seems a giant leap of faith to think that the stunning complexity of this colossal critter is the result of anything less than the work of a master Plumber, a master Artist.

God spoke all things into existence. From galaxies to glow worms, all things were created by Him. And when He was finished, He was very pleased (Genesis 1:31). When I look at elephants and giraffes and duck-billed platypuses, I feel that pleasure too.

And don't get me started on the spider. Eight legs. Eight eyes. And how does it catch its food? With a rope that comes out its bottom. Our awesome Creator has a sense of humour. And you know a spider's favourite pastime, don't you? Fly fishing.

GIRAFFIC JOKES

- Giraffes grow up to 18 feet. But most only have four.

- What do you get when you cross a giraffe with a hedgehog? A 12-foot toothbrush.

- Did you hear the joke about the giraffe? It's a long one.

- Why don't giraffes like to go to the playground? Because the monkeys use them for slides.

- How do you write a report on a giraffe? First, you get a really tall ladder...

"FOR IN HIM ALL THINGS WERE CREATED: THINGS IN HEAVEN AND ON EARTH... ALL THINGS HAVE BEEN CREATED THROUGH HIM AND FOR HIM"
(COLOSSIANS 1:16)

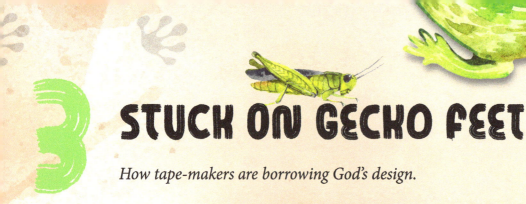

STUCK ON GECKO FEET

How tape-makers are borrowing God's design.

Humans have invented remarkable devices. Like the wheel. Computers. And the singing fish. But did you know that creation's critters have been using advanced technology much longer than we have?

The invention of sonar was revolutionary in naval warfare and navigation. But bats, whales and dolphins had been using it for eons, thanks to their Creator. In order to navigate at night, a bat lets out 190 precisely calibrated clicks per second, beyond the range of human hearing. As the bat's ears pick up the echoes, its brain translates these echoes into a precise image of the world around them. In essence, bats are using sound to see. Try this yourself when stumbling around your house at night. Okay, maybe not.

One species of horntail wasp has two needles on its backend. (Some say that needles are scary. I guess they have a point!) But the wasp has tiny drill bits which bore into a tree where the wasp deposits its young. If you've used a drill, you know you have to put some weight behind it. The horntail doesn't have enough weight to drill into a tree, so these twin drills work in tandem, pushing off and reinforcing each other like a zipper. Scientists are studying the horntail wasp so they can design drills that work in low gravity environments, like Mars and the Moon.

Geckos make me grin. Maybe you say, "But I never trusted lizards, right from the gecko." But hear me out. This little guy is helping humans build the perfect glue. It's a little off the wall, but let me explain.

For millennia, humans have been astounded by a gecko's ability to walk up walls, cling to ceilings, and stick to even the smoothest surfaces. They don't have sharp claws or adhesives or suction cups, but a gecko can support its entire body weight on a wall with a single toe. How?

Ask a gecko if you can study the bottom of his foot. He'll likely say "No." But if you find a cooperative gecko, you'll find his foot pads covered in scales. Put those scales under a microscope and you'll find clusters of tiny hairs, much thinner than a human hair. Zoom in and you'll find a terrible case of split ends with up to

1,000 nano-tips splitting off a single hair. These are called setae. A gecko's toe pads sport half a million of them, allowing those feet to hold fast to whatever he's climbing. And they never lose their stickiness. But how does this lizard wizard let go? Good question.

The tips of the setae are shaped like tiny spatulas that are sticky when they lay flat. But when the gecko moves its foot forward, the tiny spatulas lift on one side, like suction cups, and the setae disengage. Incredible.

You can now buy Gecko Tape, with nano-hairs that mimic the setae on a gecko's foot. Shouldn't God get royalties from the tape makers?

As I learn about bats and wasps and geckos, I find myself confused and amazed. Confused that anyone could believe these amazing animals just evolved due to random forces. And amazed at the infinite creativity of our Creator. Who else could engineer something as incredible as a gecko's foot?

That's my story, and I'm sticking to it.

THE GECKO GRILL

Geckos love insects and even baby mice. Here's what's on their menu:

———

Crunchy Cricket Chips (with mealworm dip)

Organic Fruit Flies

Rack of Sliced Ring Worm

Salted Ant Soufflé

Deep Fried Grasshoppers topped with minced earthworm

Dessert: Mice With Lice On Ice

———

"THROUGH HIM ALL THINGS WERE MADE; WITHOUT HIM NOTHING WAS MADE THAT HAS BEEN MADE" *(JOHN 1:3)*

11

4

SURVIVAL OF THE SLOWEST

How creation's most awkward creature manages to survive.

A dad asked, "What did you learn about in school today?" His son said, "Dragons." "Your class learned about dragons?" "Well," said the boy, "I learned about dragons. I don't know what everybody else learned."

The only thing I know about dragons is what to do when they sneeze. You get out of the way. But a real critter that seems almost as implausible as the dragon fascinates me. It is named after one of the seven deadly sins.

Nearly 300 years ago French naturalist George Buffon described it this way: "Slowness, habitual pain and stupidity are the results of this strange and bungled [creature…they are] the lowest form of existence. One more defect would have made their lives impossible."

The docile sloth lives where it's warm, spending most of its life asleep in rainforest treetops. If a sloth is in tip-top shape, it can crawl about 120 feet a day—much like a teenage boy cleaning his room. Some spend their entire lives in the same tree where they were born. (The sloths, not the teenagers.)

To reach higher speeds, a sloth will sometimes misjudge the thickness of a branch, plummet hundreds of feet, bounce once or twice, and lay there stunned. Then, ever so slowly, it climbs the tree to rest up and do it again.

And how did these awkward creatures not reach extinction? Here are just three of their design features.

1. **A sloth's movement mimics the swaying of branches.** Rainforest predators have eyes tuned to pick up movement and pounce, but the sloth is almost impossible to detect.

2. **Sloths are designed for durability.** They spend most of their lives just hanging out. Often upside-down. Try this and you can't breathe long. New research finds that their organs are fixed in place so they won't press down on their lungs. Sloths love to say, "Hang in there buddy."

3. **Slowness helps conserve energy.** An adult sloth can survive on just three leaves a day. This tree-dwelling marvel is not just a survivor, it's a thriver, precisely because it's so slow. Sloths are rarely hired as lifeguards or paramedics, but they are perfectly suited to their treetop home.

And what can we learn from them?

The Bible tells us to be quick at certain things. Quick to repent. To forgive. To listen. But we should also be "slow to speak and slow to become angry" (James 1:19). The sloth reminds us that God created His children with such variety: different backgrounds, gifts, talents, and speeds.

The French naturalist called the sloth "the lowest form of existence," but 1 Corinthians 1:27-29 says, "God chose the foolish things of the world to shame the wise; God chose the weak things of the world to shame the strong…so that no one may boast before him."

May we boast, not in our abilities, our speed or our strength, but in our marvelous Creator God. Which reminds me of the five-minute acceptance speech a sloth gave when he won an award. He said, "It's… about…time."

SPOT THE FAKE

Four of these facts are true. Can you spot the untruth?

1. Sloths are so slow that mold grows on their fur.
2. Gorillas burp when they're happy.
3. It takes sloths 30 days to digest a leaf.
4. An ostrich's eyes are bigger than its brain.
5. Giant anteaters can eat 30,000 insects a day. Yum.

The fake is #1. Sloths are so slow that algae grows on their fur. The sloth provides the algae with shelter and water. The algae provide the sloth with camouflage and extra nutrients. And everyone's happy.

SILLY SLOTH

Did you know that the sloth loves winter? Yup. They throw slow balls and make slow men.

"THE LORD IS NOT SLOW IN KEEPING HIS PROMISE, AS SOME UNDERSTAND SLOWNESS. INSTEAD HE IS PATIENT WITH YOU, NOT WANTING ANYONE TO PERISH, BUT EVERYONE TO COME TO REPENTANCE"
(2 PETER 3:9)

5 THE WOODPECKER

You need some divine intervention to survive 1,200 g's.

Did you ever hit your head on a car door? I hope not. But if you have, you know it hurts. So, imagine my surprise when I saw a woodpecker clinging to the side of a metal lamppost, slamming his beak into that metal tree. OUCH! I thought, *This is not the brightest bird in the flock. He's one feather short of a wing. How could he possibly pound his head into metal at lightning speed without one colossal headache? Without turning his brains to pudding?*

We humans can handle 5 g's before passing out. At about 46 g's our blood vessels go *KABLAM!* If we know Jesus, we'll be in heaven. Not the woodpecker. It can drum its beak up to 22 times a second without departing this earth. In a pressurized suit, a specially trained fighter pilot can experience up to 12 g's. But for the woodpecker a dizzying 1,200 g's are no problem. Without breaking a sweat or a blood vessel, it can withstand 100 times the G-force we can handle. How? A woodpecker's body comes with eye-popping design features found on no other bird. Here are just six:

The beak is composed of tiny scaly structures that pass over each other to absorb impact.

Thick neck muscles contract just before each sudden strike, diverting the force through the woodpecker's body, away from the brain.

An extra eyelid closes before impact to keep its eyes from popping out.

The tongue exits through the back of the throat, where it splits in two, wraps around the back of the skull, and attaches at the top of the beak—like a seatbelt—keeping things in place during the backswing.

The skull is a thick and spongy shock absorber for the deadly blows.

The brain is packed tightly inside the skull so it doesn't bounce around, and oriented vertically so the impact is spread over a large surface area.

The more scientists examine this fascinating creature, the more stunning features they discover. The woodpecker is perfectly designed. Part shock absorber. Part jackhammer. 100% awesome.

In fact, this superbird has no business existing unless she was crafted by an infinitely intelligent Creator with a twinkle in His eye.

A scientist was having a conversation with God. He said, "Science can do everything you can do. We don't need you anymore."

God replied, "That's an interesting theory, let's test it."

"How will we do that?" asked the scientist.

"Let's have a man-making contest. We'll start from scratch, like I did in the beginning."

"Great," said the scientist, grabbing a handful of earth.

"Hey! No cheating!" God said. "Get your own dirt."

Let me be very clear: I'm a big fan of science. God has given us remarkable brains with which to observe and decipher. But every question answered by science creates more unanswered ones, and we cannot create from scratch. Nothing comes from nothing. Until the Creator enters the picture.

Next time you see Woody Woodpecker slamming his beak into a metal lamppost, don't faint. Just smile and think about that.

SPOT THE FAKE

Four of these facts are true. Can you spot the untruth?

1. The woodpecker stabs its beak into a tree 12,000 times a day.

2. You can tell a whale's age by examining the wax plug in its ear.

3. Giraffes can pick their noses with their tongues.

4. Rats laugh while being tickled.

5. Only male reindeer grow antlers.

The fake is #5. Both male and female reindeer grow antlers. Did you think it was #3?

"...THE WHOLE EARTH IS FULL OF HIS GLORY"
(ISAIAH 6:3)

6 THE WHALE

When you're the world's largest and loudest, how do you find lunch? No problem.

Some of creation's most fascinating creatures are also its biggest. The blue whale is the largest animal that has ever existed. Period. Measuring up to 110 feet, its tongue alone outweighs an adult elephant. In fact, it weighs 330,000 pounds, or 19,400 toddlers. These monsters eat as much as 13,000 pounds of jellybean-sized shrimplike krill each day. Six teenagers can't even do that.

The bowhead whale can live more than 200 years. Scientists determine a whale's age by their accumulated ear wax. My grandkids can tell my age by my accumulated ear hair. I'm kidding. I think.

The sperm whale is a perfectly designed diver. No one knows how deep they can go, but creatures found in their stomachs are known to live three kilometers below the surface. In preparation for a dive, the whale gulps air through its blowhole, then plunges. Its secret diving sauce is spermaceti oil in the whale's massive head. These creatures were once hunted for this oil, which powered the lamps of the Industrial Revolution.

As the sperm whale descends, often for more than two hours, the spermaceti cools and condenses until it's solid. The hardened oil becomes a weight that pulls the whale downward, so deep that their lungs collapse. No sunlight penetrates these depths, so the whale navigates using a melon-like mass in their head for echolocation—releasing a rapid series of clicks. Like bats, they use sound to "see." Epic battles are fought in the darkness with their favourite prey, the giant squid. No one has seen these battles, but sperm whales sometimes return with squid beaks in their stomachs and large circular scars from the squid's suckers.

Sperm whales are the world's largest toothed-carnivore. They have the world's largest brain and make the world's loudest sound—up to 236 decibels—almost twice as loud as a jet airplane. So if you're thinking of a sperm whale for a pet, warn the neighbours. Their clicks aren't just loud, they're incredibly complex, leading researchers to believe that sperm whales may have a language more sophisticated than our own. Different clans use different languages. It's possible that a sperm whale from Iceland couldn't understand one from Australia. "Excuse me, mate! Let's slip a shrimp on the barbie."

Some are certain the sperm whale is in the Bible as the great fish that swallowed Jonah. It's the only marine creature capable of swallowing a human adult whole (the blue whale's esophagus is too small). Others say that can't happen. But I think a God who can create such mind-boggling creatures can do anything He wants. Jonah chapter 2 says that Jonah disobeyed God and took the wrong ship. When he was thrown from the vessel, God prepared a great fish to swallow him. God spoke to the fish and it vomited Jonah onto dry land. From the boat to the belly, from the burp to the beach.

In the end both the whale and its cargo, Jonah, listened and obeyed God. When I study the awesome way God designed the whale, is it so hard to believe this whale of a tale?

One more thing: You know what time it is when a whale jumps into your boat? Time to get a new boat.

WHALE OF A TALE

Scientists continue to uncover remarkable facts about whales. They now know that whales sleep in water beds. That the Orca's favourite game show is "Whale of Fortune." And British whales eat fish and ships.

SPOT THE FAKE:

Four are true. Which one isn't?

1. Killer whales are the largest members of the dolphin family.
2. Only female mosquitos bite.
3. Humpback whales only eat every three weeks.
4. Bats have thumbs.
5. Whales' tails are like human fingerprints. No two are the same.

The fake is #3. They don't eat for most of the year.

"YOU ALONE ARE THE LORD. YOU MADE...THE EARTH AND ALL THAT IS ON IT, THE SEAS AND ALL THAT IS IN THEM. YOU GIVE LIFE TO EVERYTHING, AND THE MULTITUDES OF HEAVEN WORSHIP YOU"
(NEHEMIAH 9:6)

7 THE HUMBLE BUG

Can caterpillar soup fly 3,000 miles? You'll be surprised.

In three years, Claira has experienced a radical transformation. Once prone to coating our entire kitchen table in maple syrup, this former cyclone just helped me do the dishes. "Don't leave on that trip, Grandpa," she said, hugging me tight. "Stay here. I love you."

Claira is seven and lives life in wonder. She loves bugs. She collects bugs. She talks to bugs. When Claira meets a new bug, her eyes light up like Christmas morning and she introduces it to the whole family. Her interest in the creepy crawlies has me interested, and the more she teaches me about bugs, the more flabbergasted I am.

Hearing about the planthopper causes my eyebrows to jump. When hopping, its long hind legs extend in a millionth of a second. If these legs don't fire at exactly the same millisecond, the bug will spin wildly off course, like characters in a Bugs Bunny cartoon. So how are its legs timed so intricately? At the base of each hind leg, researchers found a gear with microscopic teeth. These teeth interlock perfectly. As the bug pushes off, the gears spin at fifty thousand teeth per second, forcing each leg to move in exact unison, ensuring the planthopper a straight jump each and every time.

Claira's bug of the week is the caterpillar. This squirmy eating machine consumes many times its body weight each day. Then it hangs upside down from a twig or leaf, spinning itself a silky cocoon or molting into a shiny chrysalis. Inside its new home, the caterpillar releases enzymes that melt its tissues to mush. And then! The caterpillar soup arranges itself into new cells which group into tissues, organs and body parts. And when that new creature—that stunningly beautiful butterfly— emerges, it is nothing like the leaf-chomping worm-with-legs it was in a previous life. Guided by a brain the size of a pinhead, the majestic monarch butterfly will flutter 3,000 miles to Central America, often ending up at the same tree its parents landed on a generation or two earlier.

This great wonder of the world reflects the heart of its Creator who offers us the same thing: "...if anyone is in Christ, the new creation has come: The old has gone, the new is here!" (2 Corinthians 5:17). The process may be slow and messy, but the final product will be magnificent. And one day soon, we're gonna fly.

Before I left on my trip, Claira gave me two kisses, clasped her hands and prayed, "Dear Jesus, help the pilot not to crash Grandpa's plane into the water. And help him have a good life up there. Amen." Her love of life and her sadness at my leaving filled me with childlike wonder. So I kissed her twice and told her what is now her favourite joke: "Don't eat caterpillars. You'll get butterflies in your stomach."

LAME CATERPILLAR JOKES

Q: What do you get when you cross a caterpillar and a parrot?
A: A walkie-talkie.

Q: What do you call a caterpillar with no legs?
A: A worm.

Q: What goes thump, thump, thump, splat?
A: A caterpillar with one wet shoe.

Q: What's a caterpillar's favourite way to swim?
A: The "butterfly stroke."

"BY FAITH WE UNDERSTAND THAT THE UNIVERSE WAS FORMED AT GOD'S COMMAND, SO THAT WHAT IS SEEN WAS NOT MADE OUT OF WHAT WAS VISIBLE."
(HEBREWS 11:3)

SUPER ATHLETES

Pound for pound, insects are the strongest creatures on earth. Here are some world records:

Powerlifting Champion: The horned dung beetle. It can pull 1,141 times its body weight. That's like a human bench-pressing 180,000 pounds.

Long Jump Record Holder: The humble flea. It's able to jump 150 times its body length. That's like us leaping two and a half football fields in one hop.

World's Fastest Land Animal: The tiger beetle. Of course, it's a slowpoke compared to the cheetah. But if you consider its size, it's the fastest, topping out at eight kilometres an hour. If it were our size, its speed would reach 500 kilometres an hour.

Strongest Builder: The webbing of the Bark Spider is 25 times sturdier than steel. No man-made fiber on Earth comes close.

Nuclear Survivor: The cockroach. It may be disgusting, but it can survive a week without its head, and withstand high doses of radiation. Therefore, in a nuclear apocalypse, most countries would still have fully functioning governments. (Sorry. I couldn't resist.)

8 THE MIGHTY FLAGELLUM

Where do we find creation's most efficient motor? (Hint: It's not a Buick.)

I lived through the '60s, so very few things blow my mind. Hippos do. They fuel their bodies by eating about 36 kilograms (80 pounds) of grass each night. But cells intrigue me even more. Scientists once considered the cell little more than a bag of goo. But as microscopes improved, so did our understanding, and researchers uncovered a universe of complexity beyond their wildest imaginings. It has been estimated—get this—that there are as many working parts within a single cell as there are people on earth. And the average human is made up of 37 trillion of these cells.

And it gets wilder. Our bodies contain even more bacterial cells. That's right. You have more bacterial cells than human cells. But don't open the hand sanitizer just yet. Most will do you no harm. In fact, we couldn't survive without our bacterial buddies. They help us fight diseases, neutralize toxins, and digest food.

In one random study, 60 Americans had their belly buttons swabbed. Lurking there were 2,300 species of bacteria, 1,500 of which were unknown to science. One guy had bacteria originating in Japan, which he had never visited!

Bacteria are crammed with surprising features and equipment. Some can turn water into ice, or generate electricity. Some have guns that can shoot more than 60 molecular bullets a second to pierce the cell walls of other organisms. Still others propel themselves by firing strings at nearby objects, like Spiderman. But *the* most impressive piece of bacterial equipment has to be the flagellum. It is creation's most efficient motor.

So tiny you can't see it, the flagellum features a rotor, drive shaft, universal joint, bushings, bearings, a clutch, a braking system, and a whip-like tail that functions as a propeller. This tail can twirl at 100,000 RPM in one direction then reverse on a quarter of a turn and whip around at the same rate in the other direction. It makes a Ferrari look like a child's toy. The flagellum can propel a bacteria at 20 body lengths per second through thick gooey liquid. That's like you swimming 139 km/h (86 mph) through Jello. That's tiring and sticky work.

The scientist Michael Behe uses the flagellum to point to the existence of a Designer. If you remove a single piece of its motor, it quits. The pieces make no sense unless they're all together. How then could the flagellum possibly evolve piece by piece over time?

If the simplest living thing is incomprehensibly complex, jammed with motors not seen by the naked eye nor replicated in our finest laboratories, how could we possibly imagine it popping into existence by random chance? I applaud scientists for their ongoing study. As I marvel at the fabulous flagellum, I find myself smiling and tipping my hat to its Creator.

Hebrews 1 tells us that through Jesus, God created the universe, and He sustains and maintains it all. From the limitlessness of the solar system to the uniqueness of our fingerprints, all things were made by Him. I cannot comprehend a more logical and satisfying explanation and I cannot muster enough faith to believe in random chance.

The next time you gaze at the night sky, see a Ferrari zip by, or try to pick up a hippo, remember who holds it all together. And speaking of hippos, you know the difference between a hippo and a Zippo? One is pretty heavy and the other is a little lighter.

FIND THE BALONEY

One of these is false. Which is it?

1. Insects cannot close their eyes.

2. Sheep have four stomachs.

3. With its whiskers a cat can check if it will fit into a space.

4. 200,000 U.S. scientists identify as Christians.

5. Nine-banded armadillos always give birth to identical quadruplets.

The baloney is in #4. The number is 2 million (Christianity Today).

"FOR SINCE THE CREATION OF THE WORLD GOD'S INVISIBLE QUALITIES— HIS ETERNAL POWER AND DIVINE NATURE—HAVE BEEN CLEARLY SEEN, BEING UNDERSTOOD FROM WHAT HAS BEEN MADE, SO THAT PEOPLE ARE WITHOUT EXCUSE"
(ROMANS 1:20)

THE NOSE KNOWS

Why a little sniffer is one of the greatest marvels of creation.

Of all the critters in this book, the dog is the most loved. It is, without a doubt, man's best friend. (Sorry gals.) In my opinion, God tailor-made this perfect companion for humans.

Dogologists who study air flow to the dog's nose are bug-eyed about their findings. If you've spent ten minutes in a pig barn, you know that the stink mercifully fades. But not for the dog. Muscles deep in its nostrils draw air inside, displacing the air already there through slits in the side of the nose, constantly pulling new scents in, helping the sniffer smell. The tissue on the inside is enveloped by receptor sites, each with hairs standing guard to catch sniffable molecules. Our noses have about 6 million of these receptors, the sheepdog has over 200 million, the beagle far more.

Dogs see with their noses, like we see with our eyes.

I am an incurable snacker. Most midnights insomnia nudges me from my warm sheets. I tiptoe to the kitchen past a sleeping dog. There I stack cheese and crackers, top them with pickles, and sneak back to bed. Only a few times my wife has wakened and murmured, "Crumbs!" But not once have I fooled my dog. She smells everything. If you think a dog can't count, give him two treats and leave a third in your pocket.

The nose knows.

Through the years I've read a dozen dog books, from novels to scientific tomes. I've learned fascinating things:

- The dog must always die during the closing chapter.
- The average dog can tell which full Olympic-sized pool has a teaspoon of sugar in it.
- Dogs can hear four times the distance of a human.
- They can be trained to detect cancer and other diseases in humans.
- Dogs are the only animals that follow your point as you point out an object.
- The bloodhound's sense of smell is so reliable it can be used as evidence in court.
- 45% of U.S. dogs sleep in their owner's beds.

Canines are created for companionship. They look into our eyes and return our gaze. Try this with a chimp at the zoo and he will have a fit, viewing your gaze as aggression.

Human blood pressure goes down when petting a dog. And so does the dog's.

Dogs can get information from the mirror, but they never study themselves in one. They're that humble.

Dogs serve in hospitals, schools, prisons, nursing homes, and psychiatric wards. They help military vets with post-traumatic stress disorder.

Researchers are just discovering the tip of the tail of this complex creature. A hundred years from now, scientists won't wake up and say, "Hey! That's it! We now know everything about the dog. Let's study gerbils."

Isaac Newton, one of the most influential scientists in history, wrote, "In the absence of any other proof, the thumb alone would convince me of God's existence." I feel that way about my dog.

Faithful, loyal, devoted, and always interruptible—she is never texting or on her phone. She goes bananas when I get home. If I was half the man my dog thinks I am, I would be a saint.

"YOU ARE WORTHY,
OUR LORD AND GOD...
FOR YOU CREATED ALL THINGS, AND
BY YOUR WILL THEY WERE CREATED
AND HAVE THEIR BEING"
(REVELATION 4:11)

Doggy Morning Schedule

8:00 AM: Awake. Stretch. Go crazy. Have breakfast.

10:05 AM: Sniff around. Roll in stuff.

11:00 AM: Scratch. Chew on stuff. Bark at nothing. Yawn. Nap.

11:15 AM: Must find bones. Must hide bones in closet, behind sofa pillow, in my master's shoe.

12:00 PM: Go crazy. Have lunch.

10 OF TARDIGRADES AND HYDRAS

Nearly invisible and almost indestructible, check out these superpowers.

It's a bit freaky to learn that there are creatures tiny enough to live in our beards. But scientists with microscopes are astounded at their beauty and complexity. Let me introduce you to two of these nearly invisible neighbours.

First, the tardigrade. Otherwise known as moss piglets or water bears, they are about the size of the period on this sentence. They live on mountaintops, in deserts and ocean trenches, and inside your ears. Okay. Not in your ears. But a few thousand of them are likely within a stone's throw of your body. Despite their size, they have legs, claws, a mouth, teeth, eyes and a small tail. They look like pudgy, 8-legged gummy bears, but they have superpowers. They can:

- Lie dormant for decades, then return to normal life.
- Be pelted by enough radiation to create the Incredible Hulk.
- Outlive the lowest recorded temperature in the universe (-272° C).
- Remain unscorched at temperatures that melt plastic.
- Live without food for more than 30 years.
- Fly into space on the outside of a rocket (it's been done) and come back smiling.

But if you're worried about swallowing one, don't be. They are no match for the acid in your stomach and the human immune system.

The German pastor, Johann Goeze, discovered these little guys swimming around in his microscope in 1773. Today, scientists continue to be mystified by their marvels.

While tardigrades are the teddy bears of the microscopic world, neighbour number two is a barely visible monster with other superpowers. You'll find them in bodies of freshwater almost everywhere. The hydra has a stock that anchors itself to a solid surface. At the other end sits his head and as many as 12 tentacles armed with thousands of poisonous darts. Any unfortunate neighbour brushing against a hydra tentacle is instantly paralyzed, and swallowed whole (I hate when that happens).

If you cut off a hydra's tentacle—and I hope you won't—it will regrow into an entirely new hydra. If you cut a hydra into 100 pieces (please don't) it may cost him an arm and a leg, but in a day or two, you'll have 100 mini hydras. In one famous experiment, mean scientists plunked a hydra in a blender and pulverized it into hydra goo. The hydra didn't even yell, just regenerated into a healthy hydra. So should we run and hide? No. The batteries on the hydra's stinging cells are far too weak to affect humans.

In 1774, Abraham Trembley first noticed this animal's remarkable feats. More than 250 years later, they still remain a mystery.

As scientists peer through microscopes at the tiniest creatures, they are finding complexities that defy explanation. Apart from a creative Designer with a mind light years beyond any human's, I find no explanation either.

From the ginormous elephant to tiny creatures small enough to live in our beards, all creation declares the glory of God.

One more stunning fact about hydras: They don't appear to age, or die of old age. From what we know, the hydra can live *forever*.

Gazing with wonder at the night sky or looking wide-eyed through a microscope, we find reminders of the God who set in motion the micro and the macro. Could it be that this loving God created these tiny superpowers to remind you and me that we can love Him back for all eternity?

> "HE HAS MADE EVERYTHING BEAUTIFUL IN ITS TIME...NO ONE CAN FATHOM WHAT GOD HAS DONE FROM BEGINNING TO END"
> (ECCLESIASTES 3:11)

SPOT THE FAKE

Four of these facts are true. Can you spot the untruth?

1. Cat fleas can jump up to 60 times their own body length! We call them "itch hikers."

2. Between 1901 and 2000, 52.5% of all Nobel Prize winners in Chemistry were Christians or had a Christian background.

3. With one bite, a grizzly bear can crush a bowling ball.

4. A flamingo's head must be upside down when it eats.

5. Camels can drink 50 gallons of water in one minute.

The fake is #2: It is 72.5%. Source: Baruch A. Shalev, 100 Years of Nobel Prizes (2003).

11

THE TRUTH
BEE TOLD

*These fascinating facts about bees might just
make your brain buzz.*

After I spoke somewhere, a gentleman told me he was a beekeeper. "Bees are the most amazing creatures in the world," he said. "Look them up." His wife punched his shoulder. "With the exception of you, my dear," he said.

I took his advice and now, when I hear a bee buzzing, I smile. It is the sound of one of creation's great marvels. Did you know those wings are beating more than 190 times a second? Try that with your arms. When the bumble bee lands on one of a few hundred flowers in our yard, the buzzing changes. Because it is now chewing *bumble* gum. (Not true.) Pollen is locked inside some flowers, so the bee wraps itself around the flower and vibrates at a precise frequency, close to middle C. This passcode unlocks the pollen, which lands on the bee's body. *Unbeelievable.*

The honey bee colony is remarkably complex. The queen bee lays the eggs: about three a minute. Worker bees work. Drones mate with the queen. There are guard bees. Waxmaker bees. Wanna bees. Zom bees. (Okay, those two I made up.) Nurse bees care for the sick and injured, feeding them special types of honey, depending on the problem. If it's too cool, temperature bees vibrate to raise their body temp and warm the air. Too hot? They place water droplets throughout the hive and fan their wings to cool things down.

Where did they learn all this? Did they take a course?

A bee will produce only a teaspoon of honey in its lifetime. For a kilogram of honey (about two pounds), bees will fly three times around the world. Then use the air miles to buzz off on vacation in *Sting*-apore. (Sorry. I'll beehive myself.)

Honey bees are equipped with a special organ called a honey stomach. (Those who eat too much become a little chub-bee.) Nectar is sucked into the honey stomach, mixed with enzymes, then vomited into a honeycomb. Surprisingly, honey is one of the purest substances on earth. It has been used to effectively clean wounds and fight infections. Jars of honey have been found in ancient Egyptian tombs. "Still good," they say. "Try some in your tea."

The most curious behaviour is the waggle dance. When a forager bee discovers flowers rich in nectar, they return to the hive, gather an audience and begin to dance to country music, walking in a straight line while waggling their body, then circling back and waggling again. (I'm kidding about the music.) The waggle length indicates the distance of the nectar from the hive. The angle of the dance shows the direction of the nectar in relation to the sun. (Try this next time someone asks you how to get to McDonalds.)

Recently a child of ten asked me how little bees learn. I didn't know. She said, "From a sylla-*buzz*." Well, could it be that God created that little bee with instincts and intelligence that make us scratch our heads in wonder and applaud the Creator? To me, no other option makes sense.

Thank you God for the gift of the humble honey bee. Thank you that your fingerprints are all over creation. Amen.

PS: A guy who lives near us has 50,000 bees. His wife says he's a keeper.

SWEET TREAT

In 2015, while excavating tombs in Egypt, archaeologists found 3,000-year-old honey. It was perfectly edible. Why? High in sugar but low in water, bacteria can't grown in it. In 2003, 5,000-year-old ceramic jars of honey were found buried with a noble woman in the Republic of Georgia. It was sweet to the taste. Traditionally, honey has been used to treat eye diseases, asthma, hepatitis, wounds— even hiccups.

"EAT HONEY, MY SON, FOR IT IS GOOD; HONEY FROM THE COMB IS SWEET TO YOUR TASTE" *(PROVERBS 24:13)*

12 THE MIRACLE OF YOU

The most amazing creature alive is as close as your mirror.

An atheist once asked me, "Can you honestly tell me that you have personally experienced a miracle?" My response at the time was less than convincing, but I have a better answer now: "Have I ever experienced a miracle? The truth is: I have never not."

Let me explain myself.

The brilliant physicist Albert Einstein once said, "There are only two ways to live your life. One is as if nothing is a miracle. The other is as if everything is."

Did you know that, laid end to end, your blood vessels could circle the equator four times? That's 160,000 kilometres. Or about halfway to the moon. Not impressed yet? Then take your genetic code—which is absolutely unique to you—stretch it end to end and it will reach to the sun and back 600 times. And you will be sunburned.

Have you experienced a miracle? Put your hand on your heart.

That little heart has just one job to do. It beats. Each hour it distributes 70 gallons of blood. Walk ten miles in a day and your body got seven gallons to the mile. Weighing less than a pound, the human heart beats slightly more than once a second, 100,000 times a day, 3.5 billion times in a lifetime. During the average lifetime the human heart does enough work to lift an adult giraffe 150 miles into the air. (They hate when that happens!) And it's not just one pump, but two: one ships blood around the body, the other to the lungs. And if they aren't in perfect sync every single time, you're in trouble.

Have you ever experienced a miracle?

Look in the mirror. Scientists estimate that your nose can recognize a trillion different scents! See your eye? The retina has 100 million neurons that conduct close to ten billion calculations a second, transmitting data to the brain at 10 million bits per second.

Still unconvinced about miracles? Draw a deep breath. Waking or sleeping, you gulp and process about 4,000 gallons of air in 20,000 breaths a day. That's around 7.3 million between birthdays, and 672 million over the course of your life.

The very last verse in the very last chapter of the book of Psalms says, "Let everything that has breath praise the Lord."

Psalm 139:13-14 gives us good reason: "For you created my inmost being; you knit me together in my mother's womb. I praise you because I am fearfully and wonderfully made; your works are wonderful, I know that full well."

Are you still breathing? It's not too late to marvel at the miracles all around you: a heartbeat, a wrinkled nose, a deep breath.

It's not too late to wake up and say, "Lord, I didn't know I was breathing while I slept, but here I am. I didn't think this old world would rotate again, but the sun is up and here we are. Thank you for creating this remarkable world and its amazing critters. Thank you for creating me in your image. Help me live my days in awe and wonder at the thousands of miracles all around me."

YOU'VE GOTTA BE KIDDING!

- You are taller in the morning.
- The human eye can change its focus 50 times a second.
- Our eyes remain the same size all our lives.
- Our ears and nose never stop growing.
- When we breathe, we favour one nostril.
- You can't breathe and swallow at the same time.
- Our eyes blink about 42 million times a year.
- Every second our body produces 25,000 new cells. No kidding.

"KNOW THAT THE LORD IS GOD.
IT IS HE WHO MADE US,
AND WE ARE HIS;
WE ARE HIS PEOPLE,
THE SHEEP OF HIS PASTURE"
(PSALM 100:3)

ONE MORE CRITTER

Like millions of others, Anna Warner lost almost everything to the financial Panic of 1836.

A friend visited her one day. In the living room, Anna picked up a tiny seashell as delicate as lace and showed it to her friend. Through tears she told the friend of a time when she was sad and anxious.

Unable to pay her bills, Anna had a hard time trusting God. And then someone sent her this elegant little shell. "As I held it," she said, "I realized that if God could make this beautiful home for a little creature, he would take care of me."

And who was Anna Warner? She was the author of the world's most popular children's song. More famous than "Old McDonald" and "Baby Shark" put together. For almost 100 years, millions have sung it:

"Jesus loves me, this I know / For the Bible tells me so."

Rest assured. A God big and wise enough to create these thirteen awesome critters is good enough to love and care for us, too.

WHAT ARE YOUR FAVOURITE ANIMALS AND WHY?

List them below!

_____ _____

_____ _____

_____ _____

_____ _____

_____ _____

Printed in the USA
CPSIA information can be obtained
at www.ICGtesting.com
LVHW071030071024
793128LV00001B/2